A Mirror into
My Heart

To Angie,

Always follow that road of
happiness ~ Until you reach that
place of JOY!!
In all you do Angie, Be True 2-u!!
SHINE BRIGHT ; LIVE LIFE.

Patricia Yvonne Young

Patricia Yvonne Young

God's Love
+ Peace.   Ephesians 2:10

PAGE PUBLISHING, INC.
New York, NY

First originally published by Page Publishing, Inc. 2016

ISBN 978-1-68348-448-6 (Paperback)
ISBN 978-1-68348-449-3 (Digital)

Printed in the United States of America

Contents

Acknowledgments

First and foremost, I give all the honor, glory and the praise to my father God, for my existence!

CELEBRATE WITH JOY

I will praise you, o Lord, with my whole heart;
I will tell of all your marvelous works;
I will be glad and rejoice in you;
I will sing praise to your name,
oh most high.

Psalm 9:1-

"RESPECTFULLY" to the late Howard O. Jones, I give my deep and sincere gratitude for the many years of encouragement along with the endless publications of the Writer's Journals, given to me to spur my poetic ambition. As well as the honorable mention given to me in his autobiography, Gospel Trailblazer, which he truly was! What an inspiration and blessing through him has been given to me. Cheers, I will whistle to that!

To all who have offered their time, materials, expertise, kind and sincere words of encouragement as well as acts of love throughout the process of my poetic journey, from the first step to the present. Because of you, I have found my experience to be both enlightening and rewarding. You know who you are and the role you played. With my whole HEART, I sincerely thank you ALL for blessing me, As I seek in return to bless you.

So, now, I present to you, "A MIRROR INTO MY HEART"

Faith/Blessing!

By Patricia Yvonne Young
At some point in my life,
I made up my mind that I am naming and claiming that I am going
to be a poet.
This is my right to passage—
I am stepping out on *faith*!

I cannot see it all right now—
But I *believe* it!

I must push forward my authority of independence.

I must allow my defining moment
To be my designing moment
Because my *destiny* this will be!

A Personal Letter from the Author

Written from the actual desk of the well known poet,
HELEN STEINER RICE.
(Desk, Courtesy of Lambert Fitzgerald)

Lovingly, I dedicate each thought here in expressed to all who read this book. If any of my writings offend anyone in any way, shape, or form. Please know that this is not my intention.

My words expressed are simply a mirror into my heart.

I pray that God will use this book of poems to comfort, encourage, and ignite your inner self, being of an open mind, body, and soul; to receive a blessing through the words read by your eyes and heard by your ears, for this is my gift to you.

Remember, your life is just a journey. You are simply a foreigner passing through. You were sent by the Father because there is *much work to do*. This world will try to claim you, saying that to it you belong. But remember, you belong to the Father, and soon God will be calling you home.

Yes, right now you are in this world, but do not let this world define you. Safely tucked within Your heart is God's key to a life *brand-new*!

So, daily you must continue to carry out your Daddy's plan, reaching out and touching hearts in every way you can. Are you with me on this journey? Please tell me I am not alone. Has the Father sent you, too? To God you do belong.

To you God's joy and peace,
Patty

GOD'S TONE

Welcome

Welcome one
and
Welcome all.
You are in your Father's house.
Clap your hands!
Stomp your feet!
You are in for a heavenly treat.

We Gather

We gather here today
Dear Lord, it is in your holy name.
Touch each person represented
In a very special way.
Speak peace and give comfort
To those who need it most.

Extend your hand of mercy
To those who have lost their hope.

Shine your brilliant light, dear Father—
Radiant is your face.

Hallelujah to you in the highest!
We honor your amazing grace.

Gratefully Thankful

Gratefully thankful—yes, that's what I am.
Made in God's image and likeness,
Shaped by the Master's hand.

Melted, molded, tugged, and pulled.
Yes, dirt filled with the breath of life.
Just look at what my Father can do.

The gift of eternal life God freely gives,
Given to all who truly love God
And strive to do God's will.

Much Work to Do

My life is just a journey,
I'm simply a foreigner passing through.
I was sent by my Father because
There is *much work to do.*

This world tries to claim me,
Saying to it I belong.
I say, "I belong to my Father,
And soon God will be calling me home."

Yes, right now I am in this world,
But this world is not in me.
Safely tucked within my heart
Is the key to my destiny.

So . . .

Daily I must continue to carry out my Daddy's plan,
Reaching out and touching lives in every way I can.

Are you with me on this journey?
Please tell me I am not alone.
Has the Father sent you, too?
To God do you belong.

Use Me

You called my name.
I heard you loud and clear.

I rose to the occasion,
Knowing with you I had nothing to fear.

I let go of me and invited you to enter in.
Not fully understanding where I was going,
Or where my journey would end.

I put my faith and trust in you,
Dear Father, to use me at thy will.
Please make me an instrument.
Use me, dear Lord.
Your kingdom we must build.

A Perfect Gift

Oh, what a gift,
A *perfect gift*
We have received.

A precious bundle of joy,
Born to set us free.

There is no box to open.
There are no fancy bows.
This gift sits high and looks very low.
I will not take it back,
So a receipt I do not need.
For this gift is not just mine.
It is for the whole world to receive.

God's Loving Care

There are many things in life
Which we do not understand.
But we must trust in God's judgment,
Guided by God's loving hand.

All who have God's blessings
Can safely rest assured.
For God gives safe passage to those
Who struggle and endure.

From the mighty wings of faith
To the humblest kneel in prayer,
Take the time to trust; you are in
God's Loving care!

You Are

You are my up when I am down.
You are my friend when none can be found.

You are my right when things go wrong
You are my calm in the midst of my storm.

You are my strength when my hope is gone
You are that cover which keeps me safe and warm.

You are my Father (and my mother too).
Yes,
You are my answer when I know not what to do.

Life

As I awoke this morning
From a very deep sleep,
I embraced the precious gift of *life*
Which God has given to me.

As I took in a breath
Then exhaled it out,
I heard my Father whisper,
This is what living is really about.

I give you *life*, abundant and free.
I give you *life*, so you can praise me.
You are my child; to you I stake my claim.

I will always be with you,
Come sunshine or rain.

God's Face

Along life's toilsome journey
We often lose our way.
Moving in our own direction,
Unsure of which path to take.

Maybe I'll turn right;
To me that seemed safe.
Here I go again,
Stepping out on faith.

Oh yes, I see the horizon
How radiant is its face!
For I know this is the right way to go,
It is paved with God's grace.

I must travel wisely
Not a moment do I dare waste.
Staying away from any detours
And those signs leading the opposite way.

Continue on the right path of your journey
The one that is narrow and straight.

Vowing never to turn back,
Striving to see
God's face.

DEAR LORD

Dear Lord,
I thought of you today as I often do.
I even shared with others your wonders,
My thoughts and beliefs in you.
You are loving, caring, forgiving, and kind.
There is no question why you stay on my mind.
Through good times and bad times,
Sunshine and rain
My love for you, Father, will forever remain.

Dear Lord,
It is me, your child, once again
Welcoming you, my Savior, to please come in.
Come in, Father, teach me your way.
Lead me, guide me, show me the right path to take—
Curved, wide, narrow or straight.
I'm putting on my shoes and stepping out on faith.

Dear Lord,
When my journey has come to its end
May I please receive my crown
And slip quietly in?

With Love in the Name of Jesus

When I say, "I love you"
These three words are true.
For God has planted a love seed
To grow inside me and you.

I love you in the name of Jesus.
Yes, this is what our Father commands.

This is God's glorious message
To be shared throughout the land.

Praise be to God in the highest
For this is our Master's plan.

We must carry out this mission:
Spreading God's abundant love
In every way we can.

The Lord's Time

With a bridled tongue,
Prayer, and an open heart
Be patient
You will receive your blessing
Delivered in
The Lord's time.

Christ Is Born!

If Christ were not born
Would there be a Christmas day?
If Christ were not born
Would we gather today in this way?
If Christ were not born
Would there be a day full of food, fellowship, and play?
Or would it simply be like any other day?
Christ is born!
So we celebrate his birth.
Before you open each gift
Take time to thank God *first*.
For this is Christ's birthday party
And we are his invited guest.
What did you bring the Prince?
Do you look your very best?
God gives, gives, and gives
Because God loves us so,
Gifts in abundance
Just to see us glow.
God teaches us that it is better to give than to receive.
What will you give Christ on his birthday?
Why not start with bended knees?

Good Morning, Father

Good morning, Father,
And thank you for seeing me safely through another night.

I am blessed to see the dawning
Of a brand new day.

As I go about my day,
I pray that you would formulate my thoughts
And bridle my tongue
So I may be pleasing in thy sight.

Amen

Father, Speak

Dear Father God,

We need you to speak to our hearts:
Speak patience, when ours is short
Speak love, when we feel unloved
Speak peace, to our minds when we are confused
Speak healing, to our bodies and our souls
When we feel we can't make it through.
Speak, Father, when there are no other words to say.

Father, speak!

Angels

Angels are all around us
Lighting and guiding our way.
Filling our hearts with understanding
Of those things we cannot change.

Trusting in the Lord
And accepting God's holy will.
Even in the midst of life's storms we can say,
"Peace, please be still."

Calming all our worries,
Putting to rest all our fears.
Knowing Christ paid the price for us
When he carried that rugged cross
Up Calvary's hill.

God Is Always Near

Prayers going up in words, thoughts, and tears—
There is not a single prayer
Our Lord does not hear.

You can call God's name anytime you are in need.
God's the doctor on call for your emergency.

Morning, noon, and night
You must have no fear.

For God is omnipresent.
Yes, *God is always near.*

Christ Is Our Gift

Christ is our gift;
We are God's gift to this world.
Each one (precious)
This one (precious)
That one (precious)
Each one is God's gift to the world—
Precious in our Father's sight!

Process of Our Lives

During the *process of our lives*
People come and people go
Many leaving lasting impressions,
Others, we barely know.
Their uniqueness profoundly different
Yet their mission quite the same:
Each one making a contribution
Touching lives in so many different ways.
Walking boldly in their gifts
Guided by God's brilliant light,
Strengthening and encouraging each step
As beauty beholds the eye.

See their ray of confidence,
Feel their energies soar.
When obstacles seem to rise,
They simply walk through life's open door.

Breaking the chains of bondage
Embracing the fullness of life
Standing on God's promises.
Yes,
For God I will live
And for God I will die.

Brand-New Day

Awakened by the rising sun
Peering through the East drawn blinds
Beckoning me to get up;
Yesterday's night has now passed me by.
Up, up, up—yes, I must rise and shine.
It is the dawning of a *brand-new day*;
I am wiping the sleep from my eyes.
I put my feet on the floor,
Stretch my hands to Heaven's sky.
It is time to start another day
Another chapter of my life.

Where will I go today?
What will I do?
Who will I meet today?
Will another dream come true?

Stepping boldly into my future.
Crossing that threshold of life.
I am proceeding with vim and vigor
Proudly holding my head up high.

Journey

If you ask me where I'm going
Let me tell you where I've been.
I've been traveling this *journey* called Life
And oh, what a trip it has been.
There have been many mountain highs.
Yes, there have been valley lows.
I often traveled about with uncertainties
Unsure of which way to go.

At times, I wanted to give up.
I wanted to retire these old worn out shoes.
But a still small voice would whisper,
Continue on your journey, my dear child, you
must reach what I have only for you.
It was then I met this friend named Jesus.
Hallelujah!
He's been my inspiration and my guide.
Always showing me which way to go
When those so-called friends pass me by.
Pass me not, ole' gentle Savior,
Hear my humble cry.
While on others though art calling,
Thank you for not passing me by.

As I continued on my *journey*,
I saw a glimpse of eternity.
I could see it
But I could not touch it.
Is this what Jesus has for me?

I saw love, joy, and unity—
Oh what a beautiful sight to see:
Their cups runneth over
They were as happy as could be.
There was such a sense of freedom
Oh yes, this must be my destiny.
You see,
With age comes wisdom
Represented by each strand of my gray hair.

Yes, this is my crown of glory
For this toilsome *journey* I must bear.

Prayers

There are *prayers* answered,
Both big and small.

There are *prayers* we may often feel
Are not answered at all.

Many times, *prayers* are answered—
Many in disguise.
To see their wondrous mercies,
We must first open our eyes.

So believe in your heart
And then you will see
The Lord never forgets us.
We must simply humble ourselves and believe.

Joy and Peace

Lord, speak to our hearts;
Speak to our minds.

Fill our bodies with *joy and peace*—
Allow it to overflow in time.

A joy-filled heart and peace of mind flowing free.
Oh *joy and peace*,
You are a part of me.

Material Things

I must have this
That I cannot do without.
Oh, sistah, come see my beautiful house.

A house is not a home
If love is not there.
Just look at that material stuff everywhere.

Does that couch wipe your teary eyes?
Does that chair express how much it cares?
Will that lamp say, "I love you"
When the need is really there?

When God calls you home
Alone you must go.
All your *material things*
Yes, will all stay below.

Best Rest

At the end of a long day
Father, you give me *rest*.
As I journey through this life
Only you know what is *best*.

Trials and tribulations come;
A cross I must bear.
When my body gets weak,
Your strength is always there.

Catching me,
Holding me,
And lifting me up—
Your almighty hand of mercy
Overflowing with your loving cup.

Free of Charge

Each day is a new blessing
Given to us *free of charge*.

There is no need to buy a ticket
Nor wish upon a star.

Accept this gift from Heaven,
Count each day as a brand new start.

The going may get tough sometimes—
Just trust God to do God's part.

Father

Father, you are that burst of energy
When my energy level is low.

You are that hiding place I run to
When I need somewhere to go.

You are my water
When my well is dry.

You are that echo of laughter
Yes, that twinkling in my eyes.

You are that motivating force
When I feel I can't go on.

Father, you are that calm
In the midst of my life's earthly storm.

Puzzle

Life is a huge *puzzle*
And you are a very important piece.
Without you in God's creation,
The world would be incomplete.

You were born uniquely different
Yes, this was by design.
Crossword or jigsaw,
God's will be revealed in time.

Take for granted never
That special person you are.
You are a *puzzle* piece
In God's great creation.

How beautiful you are!

Do Not Neglect

As you travel along life's journey
Do not neglect life's golden book.

This book is the Holy Bible.
Open it daily, peek in, and take a look.

Recite some memorable scripture,
Recall a well-known verse.
There are plenty words of encouragement
And yes, the story of our Savior's birth.

For God so loved the world
God gave the only begotten son.

Jesus was born to cover our sins,
Each and every one.

You have been given life—life eternally.
Do not neglect God's holy book
For this book will set you free!

V.O.I.D.
(Validated Only in Death)

Judge me not; it is not your place.
You were not given an invitation
So please vacate my space.

Do not try to right my wrongs
Through your eyes you see.
Judge me not—do not label me.

I do not need your seal of approval
Nor am I interested in what you say.
God holds the key to my life
As I travel along my way.

Do not count me out; hold those words you have to say.
I will be judged only by my Father.
V.O.I.D. (validated only in death)
God will have the final say.

Blessed

Blessed in the morning
Blessed both noon and night
Blessed to reach out to others—
Let your little light shine.

Blessed!

Limitations

You say you have many *limitations*;
God says your *limitations* are few.
God wants to use you with your *limitations*
God has designed a mission for you.

You were not put in life's situation to be blindly cast about.
Nor are you an aimless wanderer, bound by fear and doubt.

You say you have many *limitations*;
God says your *limitations* are few.
God wants to use you—operate in your gift.
You are on God's payroll;
God has a job for you.

Life's Test A-B-C

Do not drift into a state of uncertainty,
Do not give in to those signs of distress.
Running a race filled with many obstacles
This is all a part of *life's test*.

A test not conquered by a letter grade *A*
Not settling for a *B*.
We will only pass the test of life
When it is God's face we *C*.

New Beginning

To have a *new beginning*,
Something must come to an end.
Fact leaves no room for possibility—
That is just the way it is.

The day is a precious gift—
Be patient, be open to receive and grow.

Make your own peace according to your life's beliefs
Based on who and what you know.

Rays Raise

Awakened and greeted by the sun's radiant face,
Beaming with hope and promise,
Ushering in a brand new day.

Yesterday has gone, never to return
Traveling to many places
With only a temporary stay.

Stop by, sun, and allow your *rays to raise*
Raise those in despair and depression—
Come shine and make their day.

Faith

God surrounds us with Heavenly angels
At the time we need them most.

God reveals out measure of *faith*
Before we close the door to hope.

Walking in the shoes of *faith*
Never giving in to sight.
Trusting in God's promise
God will make all things all right.

Wondrously Blessed

I am grateful and thankful
Because I am *wondrously blessed.*

Yes, made in God's image and likeness
Dressed in my Father's very best.

Bow Your Heads, Dear Saints

Bow your heads, dear saints
Humble thy selves to me.
Allow your mind to journey;
Put all your trust in me.

For I know exactly what you need.
Oh yes, I even know in what time.
Just take the time to *bow your heads*
Dear saints,
It will all be revealed in time.

Rain Down

As we set forth to do your work.
We need to feel your anointing.
We are waiting here for a blessing.
Let it fall fresh on us: *Rain, rain*
Rain down on us, King Jesus.

God's Strength

In my imperfections,
I do not have to be strong.
I am in partnership with God;
I am not walking alone.

As God leads me, I will represent
Moving forward and making progress.
Fear only gives way to *God's strength*.

POSITIVELY
THIS AND THAT

Speak Your Words

Words that heal—
Words that build us up.

Words that hurt—
Words that tear us down.

Words in our minds are just thoughts
Until they become spoken.

Words in our minds are just thoughts
If they go unspoken.

Speak your words.

It's Cold Outside

It's cold outside
But it's warm in here.

Thank you, my friends, for inviting me in.
The snow is falling, light and free.
The wind is blowing, making it hard to see.

Why are there birds that haven't flown South?
Haven't they figured this winter thing out?

Fly away, little birdies, this is not the place to be.
You are not safe, not even in the highest of trees.

So . . .

Spread your wings and fly away.
Spring is coming soon—
There will be brighter days.

I Can, I Can

I see hope where hope dares not to go.
I have faith when the answer says "no."

I believe in those things I cannot see.
I am trusting in Jesus and all his abilities.
"Can't—" that is a word unheard of to me.
There are no negative words in my vocabulary.
Drop that 't,
That word "can," yea, that be me.

I can, I can,
I keep saying to me.
I have faith
Therefore in life I know I will achieve.
I can do all things through Christ
Who strengthens me.

Fresh, Vibrant, and Unblemished

The moon and the stars say good night.
The sun greets the morning.

The thickening of the morning fog
Thinning with each passing moment.

The crispness of the morning air
As dew on the flower petals sits.

Awakened by a choir of birds
Chirping that old familiar tune.
Putting a song in nature's heart
Filled with hope and the newness of life.

Leaving behind the yesterdays
Looking toward the tomorrows—

Fresh
Vibrant
and
Unblemished.

We

Me plus you—that equals "*we.*"
You plus me equals the same, you see.

A,B,C—one, two, three.

What a perfect combination
"*We*" have grown to be.

Happy

I am *happy*.
Today are you *happy* too?
Let's put our happiness together
And see what *happy* can do.

Maybe we can bring sunshine
Into someone's rainy day.
Or perhaps lift somebody up
By the kind words we say.

Yes, I am *happy* today.
Are you *happy*, too?
Let's put our happiness together.
Let's see what *happy* can do.

Free

The leaves lightly tossed about
By the calm yet moving breeze.

The wondrous sounds of nature
Reminding us to be *free*.

The birds taking time out to perch and sing a song,
Not waiting around for an ovation
Simply spreading their wings and moving on.

See the insects we often find a nuisance
As they scurry about their way?
For they must have families too;
They cannot stop or stay.

Although we may not understand
Or appreciate the language they speak
They have a huge stake in this creation called Life,
Each one equally as important as we.

We share this place called Earth
And yes, the heavens, too.
Many have been blessed with visible heav-
enly wings, though not seen.
You have yours, too.

Music

Music is a universal language
Everybody understands

Stomp, stomp; tap, tap—
It makes you clap your hands.

Music sees no color
Prejudice it is not.

Whether boogying, waltzing, or country stepping,
The sound of music speaks to our hearts.

Rock-pop, rhythm and blues
Classical, country, and gospel, too.
Music is universal—
Music, do what you do!

Smile

I met a man today
As I traveled along my way.
Our eyes made a connection
But not a word did we say.
His *smile* I do recall
Sent warmth channeling through.
Oh what a calming feeling to the spirit
A sincere *smile* will do.
I see his physical being
But details I do not keep.
For I know he is my brother
And many more I will pass on the street.
A penny for his thoughts;
I wonder if he considered mine?
Perhaps our thoughts were frozen
In another place and time.

A *smile* is worth a thousand words,
Says that old cliché.
A *smile* doesn't cost a cent
But it will make someone's day.

Smile!

Hand Base

Place your right *hand* on the Bible.
Let me shake your *hand*.
Does your left hand know what your right hand is doing?
Place your *hand* on your heart.

Wash your *hands*.
Handouts.
Handbook.
Handful.
Handyman.
Helping *hand*.
Praying *hands*.
Hand-me-downs.
Wave your *hand*.
Lift up holy *hands* to the heavens!

OUR WAY

Good times, bad times,
We have shared them all.

Happy times, sad times,
I often recall.

I was not always right,
You were not always wrong.

Standing up for what we believed in,
Firmly not to fall.

Strong, steadfast, and immovable
Seemed to be the way.

Knowing in the end we did it—

Our way!

S.F.S.
(Struggle, Fight, and Sacrifice)

I *struggle*
I *fight*
and
I *sacrifice* too.

I even put my pride aside
More than a time or two.

Standing and fighting, not giving in,
Strong willed and determined, this battle to win.

Whether standing alone
Or with support by my side,
I know this battle will not last forever.
It will be all over
When I reach the other side.

Shades of Blue

The color of the sky
On a clear and sunny day.
The waves rushing up to the shoreline receding,
Then running away.
A bright bouquet of balloons—aqua, navy, and powder *blue*
Rising high into the atmosphere
Guided by nature's tune.

So far, so distant
I wonder what path they will take.
Dodging each cloud they meet
As they travel along their way.
Clear blue skies, roaring *blue* seas
Float on bouquet of *blue* balloons
Race to reach your destiny.

Blue jeans on a *blue* jay
Oh how silly that would be!

A *blue* mood on a stormy Monday
Is not a good start to a brand new week.
I want to see you happy, be never *blue*.
When you are asked, "How are you doing?"
Never say with *blue* teardrops,
"I really haven't a clue."

9/11: To Look Back Doesn't Mean to Go Back

"As we look back on that tragic day of Sept. 11, 2001
We must move forward armed with weapons of
love, peace, and unity."
–Patricia Y. Young
(Love activist)

"An eye for an eye, leaves everyone blind."
–Martin Luther King Jr.
(peace activist)

"You must be the change you wish to see in the world."
–Mahatma Gandhi
(peace activist)

"When we see God in each other, we will be able to live in peace."
–Mother Theresa
(Noble laureate, peace activist)

"When I don't understand something, I reach up and
hold God's hand, and we walk together in silence."
–Mahatma Gandhi
(peace activist)

"All we are saying is, give peace a chance!"
–John Lennon
(song writer, musician, peace activist)

Self

In the silence of my mind
Where thoughts never cease to race.
Mentally eliminating the negative,
Allowing the positive to take first place.

Joy, peace, and happiness are not far behind.
The mind is such a powerful thing,
No matter the place or time.

A fragile mass of uncertainties
Blindly cast about.
We often find clouded by unwanted fears and doubts.

Self must gain control; I just have to figure this thing out.
Drifting through life without direction
Is not what living is all about.

I see love approaching in the horizon
Brilliant is its face.
Oh, what a display of strength and courage,
Determined to finish this race!
I am in control; love, peace, joy, and happiness are on my team.
The positive will always out run the negative
And put the mind at ease.

The Hand Is a Terrible Thing to Waste

Put your *hand* in the *hand*
Of the man who stilled the water.

Reach out and touch somebody's hand
Make this world a better place because you can.

God's got the whole world in loving *hands*.
God's got the whole world in loving *hands*.
God's got the whole world in **mighty loving** *hands*!

I

I think *I* did
At least I thought *I* did.
Right now *I* am not really sure.
How can things we feel so certain of
Suddenly become so obscure?

Now you see it, now you don't
Could this truly be?
Where do I look to capture that dream
Within my earthly reach?

Can *I* see it, touch it
Perhaps smell its sweetness in the air?
My senses tell me goals and dreams are attainable
The mindset must take you there.

You

Stay focused on your journey
If *you* want to continue to grow.

Tell me how far is distant
In what direction will *you* go?

You control your future, yes.
You also generate your fears.

When your closeness meets your distance
Your life's journey will then appear.

B and B

Bold and beautiful
Big and bad
Bought and borrowed
Beauty and beast
Black and blue
Bread and butter
Better and best
Beg and brag
Burdens and blessings

You say you are big, and you think you are bad
You have begged and you have borrowed—
Now does that show class?

Bold and beautiful you want to be.
First you must learn to stand on your own two feet.

Black and blue days
They come and they go.
Bundle of blessings from high sent below.

Me

I just want to be *me*—
Me exclusively.
Free from all negative judgment
Trying hard to mold *me*.

I am not you.
You are not *me*.
I desire to be *me*,
Yes,
Me exclusively.

Lil' Miss Meek and Mild

Meek and mild
That is what I'm known to be.
Lil' Miss Meek and Mild
Is the name that has been given to me.
No need to argue, fuss, or fight,
Peace always shows its light.
Dressed in a sunny disposition
Sporting a memorable smile.
The name that has been given to me is
Lil' Miss, Lil' Miss, Lil' Miss
Meek and Mild.

Ends

Don't play both *ends* against the middle,
Trying to make *ends* meet,
North to south, east to west
Searching for joy and peace.

Don't play both *ends* against the middle,
Trying to make *ends* meet.
There will always be a center.
You will reach your destiny.

Ways

Your ways are not my *ways*;
My ways are not yours.

Don't put pressure on me and my life
To get me to conform.
We are individuals, uniquely different, I must add.
We can be ourselves and still walk together
Down life's winding path.

Versus

Good *versus* bad
Up *versus* down
Joy *versus* pain
Hey
There is always a way out.

God Listens

When we talk to God, we pray.
When we pray, we talk to God.
When we meditate, to silence we listen.

When we talk, pray, and meditate,

God listens!

True Vision

Surround yourself with *true* vision.
Step out on the heels of faith.

Believing in what you cannot see
Will help you to endure this race.

No need to be swift or weary
Just keep your eye on the prize.

Surround yourself with *true* vision.
Spread your wings and take flight.

Buckle Up

Buckle up for safety—
You are on life's roller coaster ride.
Take this venture seriously.
Do not let your life pass you by.

Humble

Do not mistake my confidence for arrogance:
I am truly *humble* in every way.

Sporting a ray of confidence,
Quite arrogant, one might say.

Do not mistake my confidence for arrogance
That is not me.
I am truly *humble*, *humble* indeed.

Destiny

You write your own *destiny*
With your given pen of life—

Whether printing or in cursive,
Always complete each and every line.
Some lines may be legible,
Read by the naked eye.
Some lines may be scribbles
Lost in space and time.

Yet write your own *destiny*
With your given pen of life.

Butterfly

Butterfly, butterfly
Spread your heavenly wings.
Seek that pursuit of happiness
Conquer both joy and peace.

Butterfly, beautiful butterfly,
Spread your heavenly wings.
Your colors are amazing—
An awesome sight to see.

Flavor

If your life were a flavor—
What *flavor* would you choose?

Chocolate, vanilla, with a dash of strawberry
Maybe Neapolitan will do.

Creamy caramel, refreshing mint-chocolate chip,
Perhaps a zest of lemon—bitter but sweet.

Starlight mint, what *flavor* would it be?
Maybe a rainbow of many *flavors*
Seems inviting as can be.

Your *flavor* represents your personality—
Why not make it a scoop of happiness
Drizzled with a delicious flavor of free!

You/Your

Your space!
Be *You*!
Do *you*!

Live *your* life!

EVERYTHING

You may feel you have lost *everything*,
Leaving nothing to lose.

Remember, you have your soul—
It will always be a part of you.

Material things in life,
They come and they go.
Your soul is worth much more than
Everything
Because to God your soul belongs.

N.A.P.
(Not a Problem)

Not a problem,
No need to be alarmed;
All things are possible—
Simply remember Jesus's outstretched arms.

A ray of sunshine, a gentle breeze
And abundant life is mine—
Because of what Jesus has done for me.

Shining Star

Failed relationships.
Borrowed dreams.
The short end of the stick.
What does this really mean?

Can you measure up to others' expectations?
Do you even need to try?
Are you confident in yourself?
In your skin are you satisfied?

Compromise never that special person you are
You are much too valuable.
Yes, God's blessing—
A bright and *shining star*.

I Am, I Am

I am somebody,
I am special,
I am uniquely different
In God's special way!

Life's Song

You bring me joy when we share times like this.
You make my life worth living
When I see you refuse to quit.

Each day is not filled with sunshine
Yes, rainy days, too, must come.

You just seem to keep on moving
Knowing in your heart there is
Life's song—
Songs of hope-filled tomorrows
And brighter days to come.

You just keep on moving,
Always dancing to the beat of life's drum.

FEELING BLUE?
ME TOO

Control

You *control* what I say.
You *control* what I do.
You turn my happiness into sadness.
You even *control* that too.

Sometimes

Sometimes the days seem so long.
Sometimes the nights are scary and cold.
Sometimes I feel that I can't go on.
Sometimes I just need someone to have and to hold.

Never alone, never alone,
Never alone will I be.

Because there is a special friend Heavenly sent—
Sent just for me.

So hold me tight, I truly care.
I love you, my friend.
Please say you will always be there.

Pain and Sorrow

The smile and the laughter
Fading memories only to remain.
The joy and happiness lingering in the distance—
Untouchable, unreachable,
Now unclaimed.

Pain and sorrow becoming the tenants
Filling the vacancy of the unwanted room.

The key put into the lock only to turn.
Dare not, *pain and sorrow*
So vividly clear—
Please go away.
You are not welcome here.

Caring

All I needed was for someone to *care*.
I looked all around me
But nobody was there.

I needed a friend,
Someone on whom I could depend.
Who would be there for me
'Til the very end.

Caring is sharing, loving and kind.
Caring is sometimes, so often, left behind.

I need you; you need me.
Let's join in on *caring*
and
Live in peace and harmony.

Tears

Tears of happiness, flowering free;
Tears of sorrow, oh, why must they be?

Tears of joy, yes, *tears* of pain:
Teardrops on our pillows
Others pressed against the window pane.

Yes, Jesus sees each *tear* as it falls,
For he holds the key and the answer to them all.

Just trust and believe in Christ's holy name.
It's only then you will understand
Those *tears* of both joy and pain.

Am I? I Am

Am I that person I want to be?
Am I that person you want me to be?
Or *am I* trapped inside of me
Crying out to be free?

True self goes far beyond
What the naked eye can see
Far beyond joy, pain, and agony.

One's true self runs deeper than the deepest sea.
So *I am* spreading my wings; *I am* setting me free.
I've got to know,
I've got to see,
I have to live the life destined for me.

Name

At birth, we are all given a *name*,
One we should hold in dignity
And never bow to shame.

So respect my *name*,
As I will show due respect to yours.
Belittling one's *name*
Is not a big score.

Derogatory *names* like b— —
And mother— —
Just to name a few.
The name calling drama—
It just ain't cool.

If these are expressions of pet *names* used for love,
What are your pet names for hate?

I Do What I Do

There's only one thing wrong in this relationship
And that one thing is you.
Don't look back at me to take the blame.
I only do what I do, *I do what I do*.
I may not do what I say.
This is my party.
I rule—
So you must move out of my way.

I do what I do. I may not do what I say.
Party, party, party:
I must have it my way.

Walls

Sitting in the middle of the room
Surrounded by four *walls*—
One *wall* giving way to escape.
If you hear that hastened call.
Hear the sounds around you,
Echoing through your ears
Sitting in the middle of the room,
Thoughts so distant, yet so near.

Unseen Is Unsaid

Don't make up stories about what I do.
Telling lies and spreading rumors
Seem to be an occupation to you.

Working part time, full time,
And overtime too.
Never minding your own business;
You are an expert in gossip—
That is all you seem to do.

Get a new job, tame your tongue too.
Remember
Unseen is unsaid—
Don't make up what I do.

Feeling

I had this *feeling* today
A *feeling* I never experienced before—
It scared me, as my heart sank,
Sinking beyond the ocean's floor.

Challenge

I *challenge* you from this day forward
To not shed a tear—
Be strong, stand firm,
Turn off your listening ears.
Often the less heard
Means less said.
It's when you allow hurtful messages in,
Tears flow everywhere.

Tally

One day of happiness
Followed by three days of pain.

The scale appears unbalanced:
One, two, three days still remain.
Tally, tally, tally—
Who will win this game?

FROM SUNRISE
TO SUNSET

I Will Rise

I *will rise* high above the clouds
Where pain and suffering will never be found.

I will elevate to a higher plane
Where I will feel no guilt nor shame.

Gracefully soaring, strong and free—
Faithfully guided by the spiritual essence of me.

We Will Reunite Someday

I haven't left you; I've simply gone away.
Temporary is our separation.
We will reunite again someday.

With you, I leave my love.
Yes, special memories too.

Hold these treasures near and dear
And allow them to comfort you.

When This Battle Is Over

I fought a tough battle
You were there by my side.
Sharing tears of concern
And often the question "Why?"

Your strength was amazing
The strength God gave to you.
Now trust in God's peace and comfort.
Yes, God will carry you through.

R.M.A.
(Remember Me Always)

I am that passing breeze
Calming all your fears.

I am that sweet whisper
Traveling softly through your ears.

I will always be with you
As you go about your days.

I am that cherished memory
No one can take away.

Life Is Our Journey
Tucked in Between

My sunrise has met my sunset,
My soul is now at peace.

I've reached that light at the end of the tunnel
Where Jesus waits for me.

I leave with you, my love
Yes, special memories too.
Hold these treasures near and dear
Allow them to comfort you.

Trust

My work here has been completed
Though painful it may be.
Trust
God's peace and comfort will follow
To turn your battle bitter sweet.

Yes, there is sorrow
And tears flowing free.
Trust
In our Heavenly Father
And the new life God has for me.

Rest Assured

We know not the time
Nor what the situation may be.
We can only *rest assured*
That Jesus has come back for me.

With little or no time given
To close life's earthly door.
Leaving behind unanswered questions
Followed by more and more.

Grieve, I know you must.
Yes, the pain is real and deep.
Trust the mourning period will end
Because God has set me free.

J.E.S.U.S.

Just trust in God's unchanging promise
Of
Everlasting and abundant life
As
Sunrises mark our earthly beginnings
Gracefully
Unveiling their brilliant light
While untimely
Sunsets cast their shadows, yet giving way to
a
brand-new
life.

This Is Not a Goodbye

This is not a goodbye
Nor am I saying, "So long."

The parting of our way is only a bridge
Leading me safely home.

I conquered this earthly journey
I have come to the end of the road.

I am waiting for you in eternity
I will never leave you alone.

God's Claim Check

I have returned to the Father who sent me
God's claim check has been cashed in.

It was my turn to receive God's glory
A new life I must begin.

With me, I took your love—
That love that carried me through.

I am now with my Heavenly Father
Watching and praying
As God's love carries you through.

At Last

I am now in the light of God's presence
God has given me sweet rest.

I have embraced the fullness of God's joy
I have passed life's earthly test.

Pain, trials and tribulations
Are now things of the past.

Joy, love, and peace are truly mine—
Truly mine,
At last.

Faithful and True

Father, I am now in your presence.
I have embraced the fullness of your joy.

Your love for me is an investment
With even a far bigger reward.

God has smiled energy down on me
God has smiled energy down on me
God has smiled amazing energy down on me

Faithful and true.

In Glory

I have returned home to my Father who sent me
Which was destined to be.

God has fulfilled our prescheduled date in *glory*
According to life's will for me.

The table is wonderfully set.
Peace, love, and joy are our feast.
Surrounded by a choir of angels
As I bow at the Master's feet.

Rise

I will *rise* high above the clouds,
Where pain and suffering will never be found.

I will elevate to a higher plane,
Where I will feel no guilt nor shame.

Gracefully soaring strong and free,
Faithfully guided by the spiritual essence of me.

As I *rise*, elevate, and soar
To the past I realize I must close the door.

New life and new beginnings
are my welcomed guests.

Praise be to God—
I have passed life's test.

FAMILY

Family is a union we are all born into
Not by choice nor decision
But by what God has deemed destined to do
There are small families, there are large families
Coming in different shapes and sizes too
Family represents a beautiful ray of my colors
Far beyond red, white, and blue.

Some families are tightly woven
Others are loosely knit
Often separated by absence, time, and distance
Yet, the fact of family still exist.

There are singles, couples, and children
Yes, there are many relatives too
Some connected through the blood line
Others through marriage when two profess, "I do"

Family is a tree growing and bearing many fruits
Fruits beaming with beauty and uniqueness
Representing generations through and through

Souls journeying on leaving treasured memories behind
Captured and stored in the hearts of loved ones
Passed down through the family line
So embrace the gift of family
Both present, future, and days gone by
Count each day as a brand new blessing
We are family
Yes, you and I

Patricia Yvonne Young

Mother, Auntie and Grandmother

(A Special Dedication)

My *mother*, my *auntie*, and my *grandmother*, too
Golden nuggets, pearls of wisdom
And what it means to be a lady
I was taught that, too.

How did these three ladies hold it down?
A little spunk, much beauty, and being heavenly bound.

Their struggles were many
Yet rising above them all.
Blood, sweat, and tears
I imagine often called.
Vowing never to give up
Mixing life's bitterness with God's sweet
Keeping their eyes on the prize
Never giving in to defeat.

My *mother*, my *grandmother* and my *auntie* too,
Taught me to love and to honor God
With all my heart and in return,
In life, God will carry me through.
I Love You
Resting in Peace!

Lizzie, Glanner and Bertha

Float On

(In loving memory of my mother, Lizzie Young-Bryant)

Float on, dear Mother, feel free to fly.
No more pain,
No more suffering—
All that has died.

Spread your wings,
Sweet angel,
You have reached your Heavenly Home on High.

Feel free,
Feel free,
Feel free to fly.

In Memory of John H. Bryant
(My Stepfather)

You loved life, and life loved you,
Whether fishing, gardening,
or working on a car or two.

Caring, helpful, stubborn, and kind—
Those are the memories you left on my mind.

I think of you often
and in my own selfish way,
Wish God would have chosen
to allow you to stay.

I know you are in Heaven,
preparing a place for those you loved.
Rest on, Dear John,
It was a long and tiring road.

A Mother's Love

I loved you all, for each of you I cared.
My memory I left behind, for you my children to share.
I had no favorite,; I loved not one any less.
My dream as a mother was only to see,
You, my children, do your very best.
To want the best, to be the best, must be
the goal you strive to reach.
For life is filled with many obstacles, you will often fail to see.
Be strong my child, stand straight, do not sway.
Storms will rise;, your faith not to stray.
Remember, life is our test from beginning to end.
Always be of good courage, never to give in.
For I am with you whether you rise or fall,
A Mother's Love will be there through it all.

Strong

I am trying to be *strong*
For I know I must be:
I have two little children depending on me.

We loved you so much,
Together we grieve.
Your presence we miss—
Karen, Alesha, and me.

Your *strong* hand,
Your tender touch.
Your *strong* voice
In our hearts will never hush.

Blessed to be a Blessing

By Patricia Young

Step out on faith
You don't have to see the entire staircase
Just step out on faith.
At some point in my life, I made up my mind that I am naming
And claiming that I am going to be a poet
This is my right to passage.
I am glad and blessed, because I stepped out in faith!
I must push forward my authority of independence.
I must allow my defining moments to be my designing moment.
Because my destiny this will be!

To my family

To Ted Wilson, the love of my life and best friend. Words will never be able to express how I truly feel about you. Your undying love, encouragement, and support have no doubt been the wind beneath my wings. Ted, because of you, this book has become a reality. It was you, Ted, who encouraged me to submit my book of poetry to Page Publishing, Inc. You gathered all the information and presented it to me. Now, look. A Mirror into my HEART. I thank and love you for that. Because of you, I not only believe, but I know I can fly. Teddy, thank you for a wonderful life. To you I pledge my everlasting love.

To our daughters Tarnisha, Karen, and Alesha. You are a blessing from God's well of love. I pray; I have given you the Christian foundation, equipping you for life's many up's and down's. Mother to daughter, woman to woman, I love you and pray for God's joy, peace, and happiness in your lives of your mates, my grandchildren, present and generations to come.

Especially to you Alesha, a very special thank you for assisting me in the setting up and typing of this book of poetry. Your patience and time spent has helped this dream become a reality. I never took one moment of your time for granted. "Dreams do come true."

A very special thank you to Matt Johnson and
the entire Page Publishing Family.

Your time, patience and expertise which you have given to me
throughout the process of the birthing of *A Mirror into my HEART,*
has given me much joy and appreciation. You are the best!

I am both thankful and grateful.

Patricia Yvonne Young

About the Author

Patricia Yvonne Young defines herself as a child of God and an heir of God's amazing grace! Born and raised in the city of Oberlin and the state of Ohio. Fact: Oberlin is a city which rightfully claims much rich history and abundance substance. Yet, not exempt from life's many perils as experienced by other cities. Oberlin, one might say, "Quite Quaint".

Patricia vowed to make it her home, which she did. A daughter, a sister, wife, mother, related to many, a friend to others. Patricia enjoys writing poetry, dance, music and marvels at God's Great Creation. As Patricia journeys through this life, she desires that her message be, we are all God's children. Yes, precious in God's sight. All born with an awesome Godly purpose! Like her, love her, dislike her, hate her. No worries. Life goes on. Patricia most often called, "Patty" fully understands that she is not of this world, a foreigner passing through. Her prayer is, that the work she has done throughout this entire journey fulfills her Godly purpose. Reaching out and touching the hearts and lives of others- in a Christian way.

Conclusion:
"May the work I have done speak for me!"

Lovingly,
Patricia "Patty" Yvonne Young

CPSIA information can be obtained
at www.ICGtesting.com
Printed in the USA
LVOW12s1602121216

516922LV00002B/582/P

9 781683 484486